How to personalize this book for your Dear Daughter!

Original cover

Tools needed: (all are available at a scrapbook supply store and/or craft store)

- Acid-free glue stick
- Photo mounting squares/tape
- Scissors or photo trimmer
- Fine point writing pen (acid-free, light-fast, waterproof, fade-proof, smear-proof and non-bleeding)
- Acid-free paper for writing additional notes/letters

Dear Friends,

We created this book to be a precious keepsake for daughters of all ages. Given that some of us are "craftier" than others, we designed it so you can add as much or as little personalization as you'd like. Take a look at some of the ways you can add your own special touch...

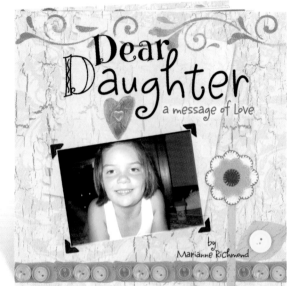

Customize the cover photo

Slip out the cover insert and paste your special photo in the indicated area. Instantly, you transform this book into something especially for YOUR daughter!

Cover personalized with photo

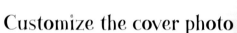

Paste your photos over ours!

One of the easiest ways to make this book your own is to gather your favorite family photos and paste them over the ones we show. Some spaces are a traditional 4 x 6 size; others are circular or sub-sized. For the cleanest cuts, you would want to use a photo trimmer (see above).

Page personalized with photos, memorabilia and writing

Tuck a heartfelt message into the vellum envelopes on pgs. 18 and 23

What are your hopes and dreams for your daughter? How much do you cherish her? Tell her in your own words and place your note in one of two special envelopes.

Page personalized with photo, fortune and letter in pocket

Affix to pages mementos of special memories, i.e., school photos, ticket stubs, postcards, etc.

Has your daughter grown into a beautiful girl or woman? Showing a progression of time can be a wonderful addition to a page.

Page personalized with photos on colored paper and writing ages on flower stems

Handwrite your own thoughts or advice on pg. 35

What words of wisdom would you like to share with your daughter? You can certainly add your anecdotes to any page. We have, however, built in a special page for "mom's advice."

Page personalized with personal note of advice and fortune

Dear Daughter

a message of Love

by
Marianne Richmond

Dear Daughter
a message of Love

Library of Congress Control Number: 2005907883

A special thanks to the creative companies whose papers we incorporated into our designs: daisyd's, Karen Foster Design, Design Originials, Making Memories©, K&Company LLC, C.R. Gibson, Masterpiece Studios.

Marianne Richmond Studios, Inc.
420 N. 5th Street, Suite 840
Minneapolis, MN 55401
www.mariannerichmond.com

ISBN 09770000-6-0

Illustrations by Marianne Richmond

Book design by Sara Dare Biscan

Printed in China

First Printing

Dear _____

_____

_____

_____

Love,

_____

Dear Daughter,

You **truly** are a
dear daughter.

PreCious
and
beautifuL.

Perplexing.
Sensitive.
Strong.

and very

giggle

funny

How Lucky I am to have the gift of you in my life.

I love watching
you **grow**

and change

and discover.

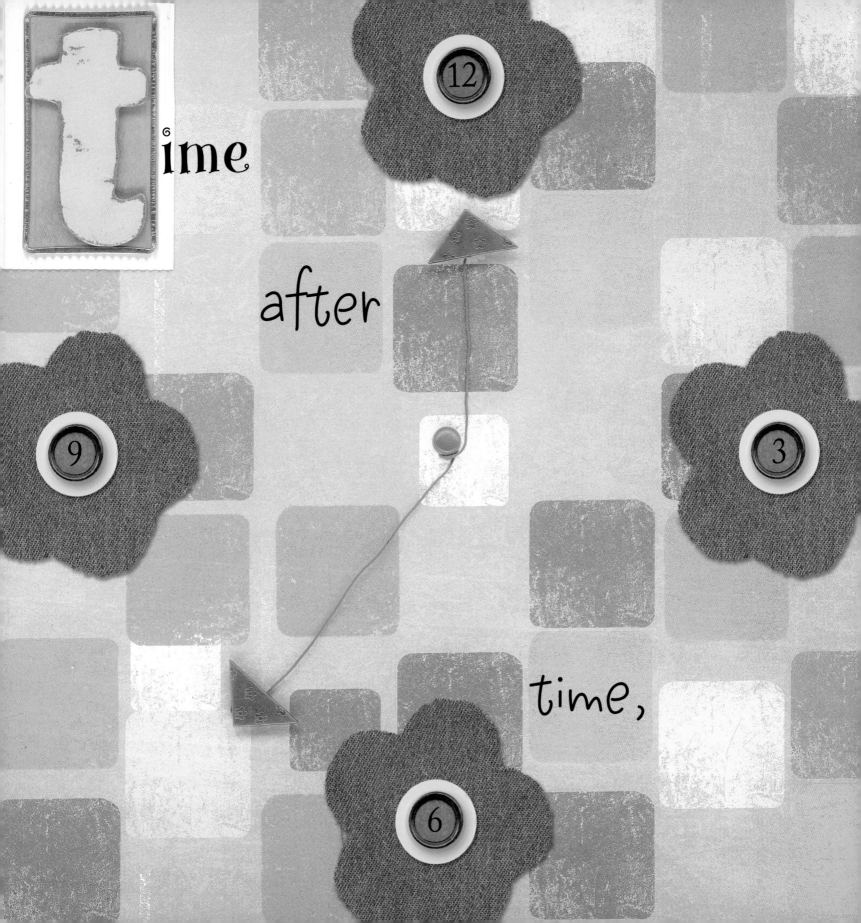

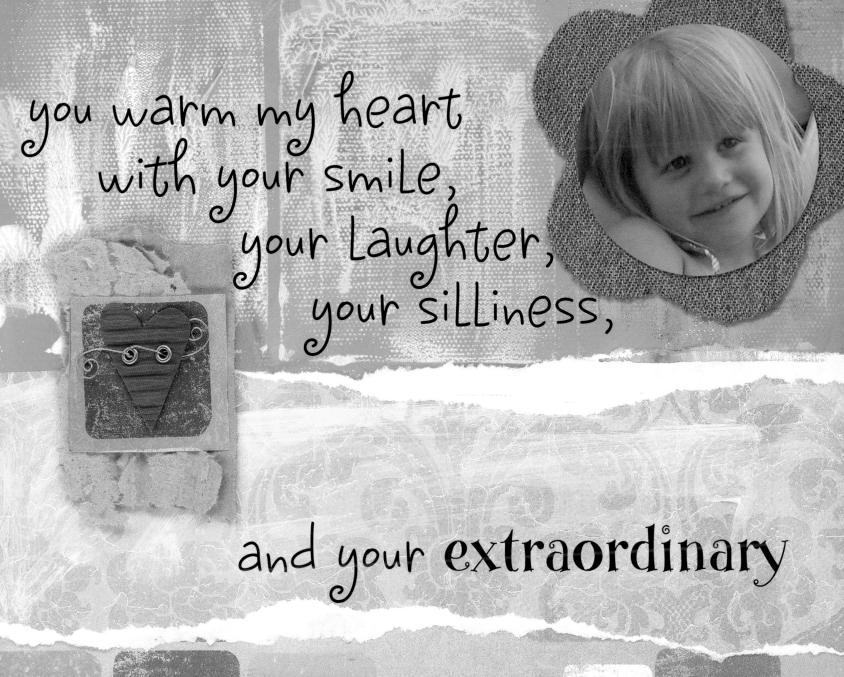

you warm my heart
with your smile,
your laughter,
your silliness,

and your **extraordinary**

I N D I V I D U A L I T Y .

I

A

M

P₃ U₁ Z₁₀ Z₁₀ L₁ E₁ D₂

sometimes, about **how** to best parent your "female-in-progress" emotions and needs.

Do you know **how incredible** you are?

wonderful life **adventures**,

Weather Low: 54
High: 8.

HIGHLIGHTS
ONGOING EVENTS

forever kind of **friendships**

and **opportunities** to pursue
your greatest passions.

Rue F
Rue Du Roule
Rue Des Halles
Rue Jean Lantier
Rue Saint-
orges Pompidou   Quai Du Louvre
Quai De La Cors
Quai Malaqua
Rue De Lille
Université   Rue Visconti
Rue Jaco
La Seine
L'Abbaye
Paris   Hôpital
Hôtel-Dieu
Île De La C
Rue Suger
Rue Xavier Privas
Rue Du Jardinet
fun
Guisarde   Rue Pierre
Rue D
Sulpice

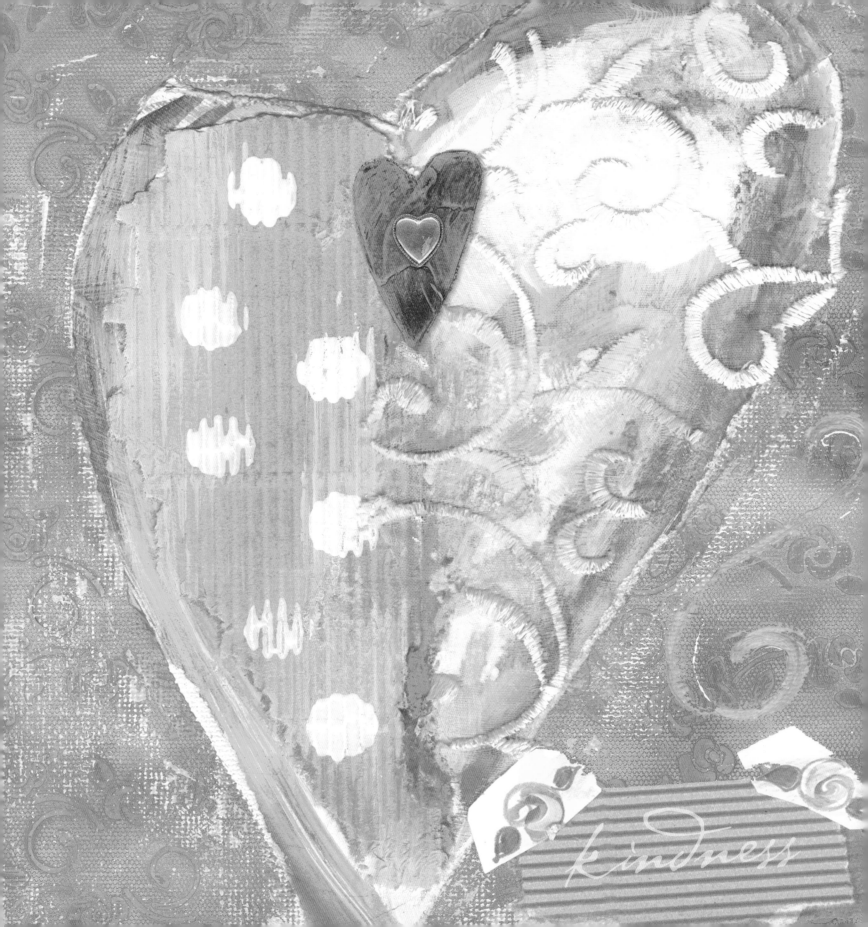

kindness

that appears at regular inter...
...entific *journal* >
syn magazine, newspaper, organ, periodical, review
journey *n* passing or a passage from one place to another
<at that time it was a four day *journey* from Boston to
New York> <she was tired though their *journey* was barely
begun>
syn expedition, peregrination(s), travel(s), trek, trip; com-
pare TRIP 1
rel excursion, jaunt, junket, sally, tour; cruise, voyage;
pilgrimage, progress, safari
journey *vb syn* GO 1, fare, hie, pass, proceed, ||process,
push on, repair, travel, wend
jovial *adj syn* MERRY, blit... blithesome, festive, gay,

JOURNEY

My heart aches when
I see you sad or hurting.
I don't know if you know
how often I pray for you...
for your
guidance
and wisdom
and
protection.

I realize we don't get along all the time

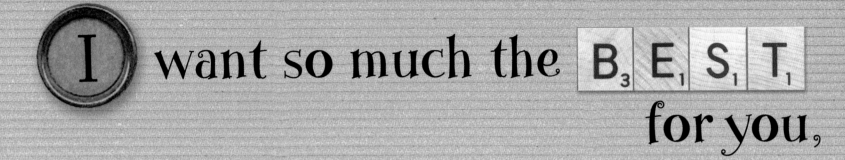

I want so much the BEST for you,

and it's hard for me to let go sometimes. To let you choose, explore, experience, and, at times, regret. My LOVE for you is just that great.

You've heard people say, "**like mother, like daughter.**" Sure, I see part of me in you... but I'd be more flattered if people saw part of you in me.

HUG

I'm so

PROUD

of you

for who you are.
I want you to feel
proud of you, too.

I TRY not to give "**motherly advice**," but can I just mention a couple things?

Take the high road as often as possible.

Let go of anger.

Think twice before you talk... or send e-mail.

LISTEN UP

THREE PERSPECTIVES

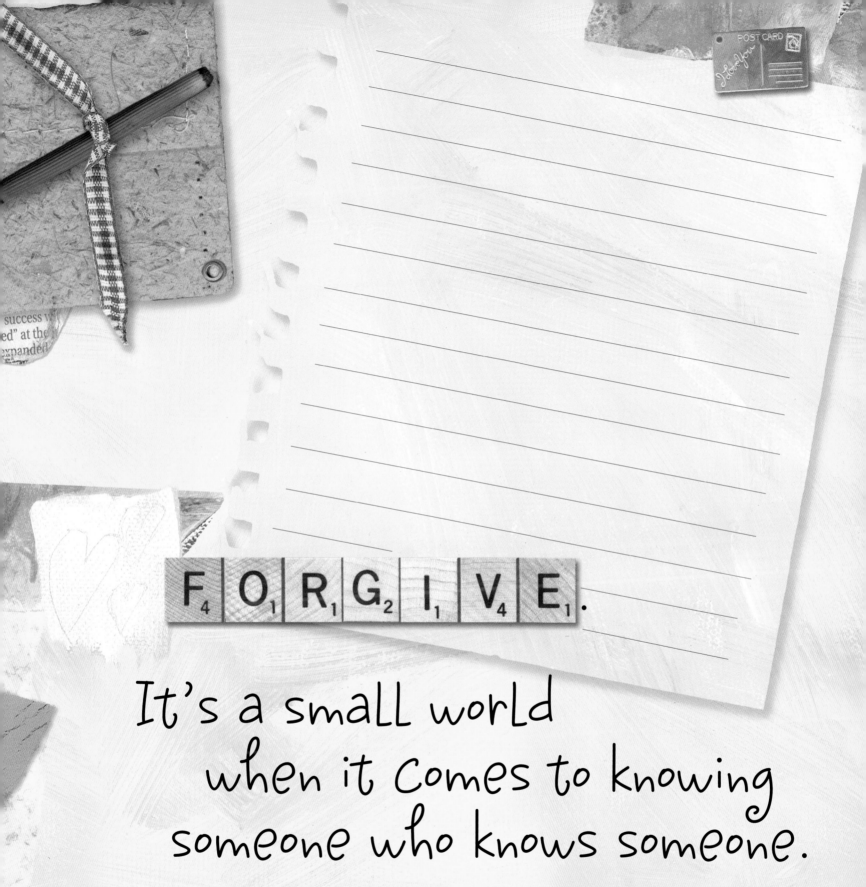

FORGIVE.

It's a small world
when it comes to knowing
someone who knows someone.

And when
you think

?

see eye-to-eye

COMFORT

I can't possibly
understand,

I'M HOME

Welcome

I
hope
you
realize
that
I
just

might.

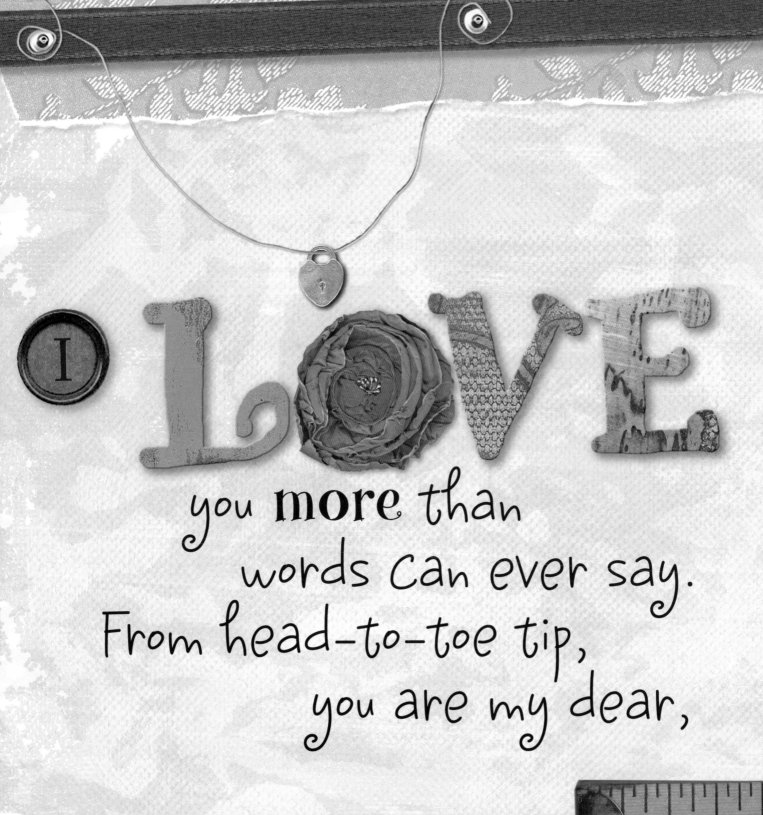

I LOVE
you **more** than
words can ever say.
From head-to-toe tip,
you are my dear,

dear daughter.

This book is **dedicated** to beloved daughters everywhere, especially Julia and Lily.

MarIANNE RIChmOND

A gifted author and illustrator, Marianne Richmond lives in Minneapolis, MN with her husband, four children and one dog... and certifies that motherhood is indeed her most humbling creative challenge to date!

Marianne continues to create products that help people connect with those who mean the most to them. Her repertoire includes books, stationery and giftware.

www.mariannerichmond.com

Marianne shares her unique spirit and enchanting artwork in her other titles:

The Gift of an Angel
The Gift of a Memory
Hooray for You!,
The Gifts of Being Grand
I Love You So...
My Shoes Take Me Where I Want to Go
Dear Son

Plus, she now offers the **Simply Said** and **Smartly Said** mini book titles for all occasions.